Gross History

Gross FACTS About

VIKINGS

BY MIRA VONNE

raintree

a Capstone company — publishers for children

Raintree is an imprint of Capstone Global Library Limited, a company incorporated in England and Wales having its registered office at 264 Banbury Road, Oxford, OX2 7DY – Registered company number: 6695582

www.raintree.co.uk
myorders@raintree.co.uk

Edited by Mandy Robbins
Designed by Philippa Jenkins
Picture research by Wanda Winch
Production by Steve Walker
Printed and bound in China.

ISBN 978 1 4747 5218 3
21 20 19 18 17
10 9 8 7 6 5 4 3 2 1

British Library Cataloguing in Publication Data
A full catalogue record for this book is available from the British Library.

Photo Credits
Bridgeman Images: © Look and Learn/Private Collection/English School, cover, © Look and Learn/Private Collection/Oliver Frey, 13, © Look and Learn/Private Collection/Peter Jackson, 9, Photo © O. Vaering/Private Collection/Peter Nicolai Arbo, 29; Capstone, 16-17; Granger, NYC – All rights reserved/Sarin Images, 15; JORVIK Viking Centre, York Archaeological Trust for Excavation & Research, 21; National Geographic Creative: Michael Hampshire, 11; Newscom: akg-images, 5, Photoshot/Martin Zwick, 25; North Wind Picture Archives: Gerry Embleton, 7; Science Source: Mikkel Juul Jensen, 23; Shutterstock: irin-k, fly design, Juan Gaertner, 27, Milan M, color splotch design, monkeystock, grunge drip design, Protasov AN, weevil, lice, parasites, Spectral-Design, 8; Thinkstock: Dorling Kindersley, 19

CONTENTS

Raiders from the sea

The Vikings terrorized Europe for nearly 300 years. These raiders from Scandinavia attacked anywhere they could sail. Their ships would appear without warning. They **looted** towns and captured thousands of slaves.

loot take treasure from a ship or town

Gross Fact

A single Viking ship could carry about 24 heavily armed warriors. Often there was more than one ship in a raid.

Wild warriors called berserkers were especially feared. Before battle they chewed on shields and ate their own skin. Even with wounds gushing blood, berserkers kept fighting.

Gross Fact

Berserkers did not wear armour or helmets. Instead, they covered their bodies in animal skins.

Terrible attacks

Vikings often faced well-armed enemies. Wounds were nasty and deadly. Iron swords sliced at chests, arms and legs. A strong blow from a sword or **battleaxe** could split a person's head open.

battleaxe weapon consisting of a wooden handle with a heavy, sharp blade on one end

Some Vikings would celebrate a victory with a feast on the battlefield. They set up their cooking fires among dead bodies. The fire cooked their food over the burning bodies of their enemies.

Tough travels

Travel on Viking **longships** was tough. Warriors had no protection from the weather. Constantly being hit with seawater made skin break out in sores. The salty water stung and kept the sores from healing.

longship long wooden boat that could be powered by sail or oar

Gross Fact

Crews spent long hours bailing out water from their ships. Sometimes their efforts weren't enough. Many Viking ships sank.

Viking **cargo** ships were higher and wider than longships. They were also crowded and smelly. Animals and passengers used the ship as a toilet. There was nowhere to go to escape the smell.

cargo describes a type of vehicle that carries goods

The food onboard could be as rough as the seas. Nothing was cooked. The risk of starting a fire on a wooden ship was too great. Tough dried meat was washed down with **lukewarm** water or sour milk.

lukewarm just slightly warm

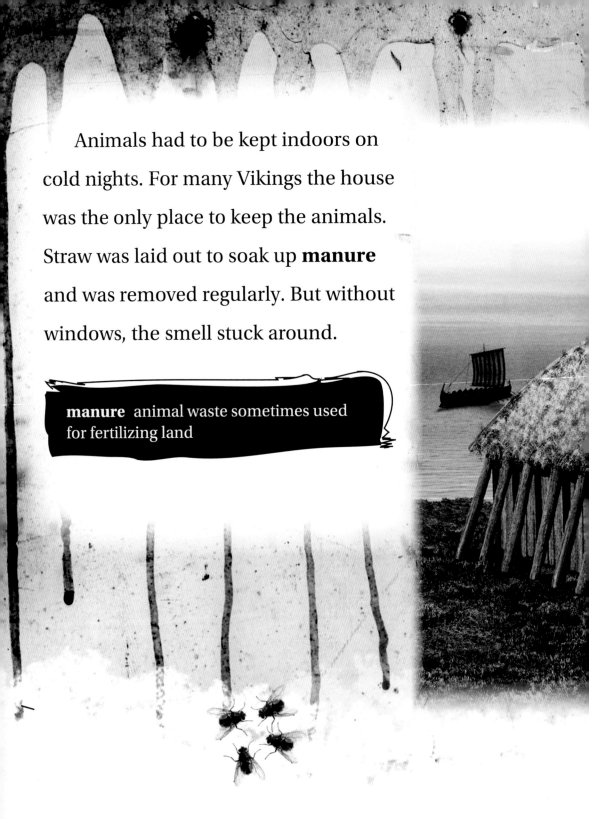

Animals had to be kept indoors on cold nights. For many Vikings the house was the only place to keep the animals. Straw was laid out to soak up **manure** and was removed regularly. But without windows, the smell stuck around.

manure animal waste sometimes used for fertilizing land

A sour supper

Vikings often **fermented** their meat. Doing this kept **bacteria** from growing. It made food last longer too. Vikings would bury an animal in a pit and leave it to sour. Shark meat and whale blubber were commonly used.

ferment preserve food in a way that prevents organisms from growing

bacteria very small living things that exist all around you and inside you; some bacteria cause disease

Gross Fact

The national dish of Iceland is fermented shark meat called hákari. It was a staple of the Viking diet.

Painful problems

Vikings had no doctors. To stop bleeding, they rolled hot iron over wounds. This painful process prevented **infection**. Other health threats were lice, fleas and tapeworms. Tapeworms caused illness and even brain damage.

infection disease caused by germs

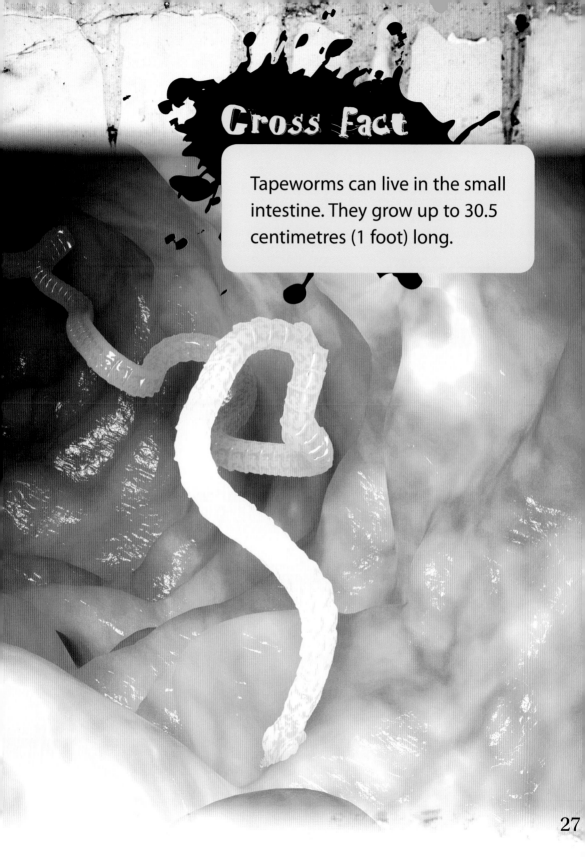

Gross Fact

Tapeworms can live in the small intestine. They grow up to 30.5 centimetres (1 foot) long.

The end of the Viking Age

In the 1060s European countries built stronger armies to fight the Vikings. It grew harder for the Vikings to raid villages. Many settled down to farm and trade. Eventually the violent Viking way of life died out.

Glossary

bacteria very small living things that exist all around you and inside you; some bacteria cause disease

battleaxe weapon consisting of a wooden handle with a heavy, sharp blade on one end

cargo describes a type of vehicle that carries goods

ferment preserve food in a way that prevents organisms from growing

infection disease caused by germs

longship wooden boat that could be powered by sail or oar

loot take treasure from a ship or town

lukewarm just slightly warm

manure animal waste sometimes used for fertilizing land

Scandinavia northern European countries including Norway, Sweden, Denmark and sometimes Finland, Iceland and the Faeroe Islands

Read more

The Gruesome Truth About The Vikings, Jillian Powell (Wayland, 2012)

Vicious Vikings (Horrible Histories), Terry Deary (Scholastic, 2016)

You Wouldn't Want to be a Viking Explorer!: Voyages You'd Rather Not Make, Andrew Langley (Book House, 2014)

Websites

jorvik-viking-centre.co.uk/who-were-the-vikings/
This website has information about Vikings and how they lived.

www.bbc.co.uk/education/topics/ztyr9j6
Visit this website to find out more about the Vikings – who they were, where they came from, the weapons they used and how they fought at sea.

Comprehension questions

- The details in this book are gross. What other words can you use to describe this period in history?

- How do the images add information about the Vikings? Describe some of these images.

- Compare living during the time of the Vikings with living today. Would you want to live during the 1000s? Why or why not?

Index